Heart and Blood

Injury, Illness and Health

Carol Ballard

www.heinemann.co.uk/library
Visit our website to find out more information about **Heinemann Library** books.

To order:
☎ Phone 44 (0) 1865 888066
🖹 Send a fax to 44 (0) 1865 314091
🖥 Visit the Heinemann Bookshop at www.heinemann.co.uk/library to browse our catalogue and order online.

First published in Great Britain by Heinemann Library, Halley Court, Jordan Hill, Oxford OX2 8EJ, part of Harcourt Education.

Heinemann is a registered trademark of Harcourt Education Ltd.

© Harcourt Education Ltd 2003
First published in paperback in 2004
The moral right of the proprietor has been asserted.

Editorial: Nick Hunter and Catherine Clarke
Design: Jo Hinton-Malivoire and
Tinstar Design Limited (www.tinstar.co.uk)
Illustrations: Jeff Edwards
Picture Research: Maria Joannou and
Su Alexander
Production: Viv Hichens

Originated by Ambassador Litho Ltd
Printed in Hong Kong, China by
Wing King Tong Company Limited

ISBN 0 431 15715 4 (hardback)
07 06 05 04 03
10 9 8 7 6 5 4 3 2 1

ISBN 0 431 15722 7 (paperback)
08 07 06 05 04 03
10 9 8 7 6 5 4 3 2 1

British Library Cataloguing in Publication Data
Ballard, Carol
Heart and Blood. – (Body Focus)
612.1
A full catalogue record for this book is available from the British Library.

Acknowledgements
The publishers would like to thank the following for permission to reproduce photographs:
Corbis p. **35**, Corbis Bettmann pp. **24**, **25**; Corbis Stock Market pp. **13** (David Stoecklein), **18** (Pete Saloutos), **31** (John Henley); Mediscan p. **22** (left); Science Photo Library pp. **5**, **7** (Simon Fraser/Newcastle General Hospital), **14** (Adam Hart-Davis), **16** (Bisp Beranger), **17**, **28** (Alex Bartel), **29**, **33** (Juergen Berger/Max-Planck Institute), **36**, **38** (St Bartholomew's Hospital), **40** (Astrid & Hanns-Frieder Michler), **42** (Jackie Lewin/Royal Free Hospital), Stone (David Madison) p. **12**; Steven Kahn p. **22** (right).

Cover photograph of a colour X-ray image of a human heart reproduced with permission of Science Photo Library.

The publishers would like to thank David Wright for his assistance with the preparation of this book.

Every effort has been made to contact copyright holders of any material reproduced in this book. Any omissions will be rectified in subsequent printings if notice is given to the publishers.

CONTENTS

Words appearing in the text in bold, **like this**, are explained in the Glossary.

The heart is a vital organ, pumping blood around our bodies every minute of every day of our lives. Blood is the body's main transport system, carrying oxygen and **nutrients** to tissues and removing waste products. Without a constant supply of blood, none of our organs would function and we would soon die.

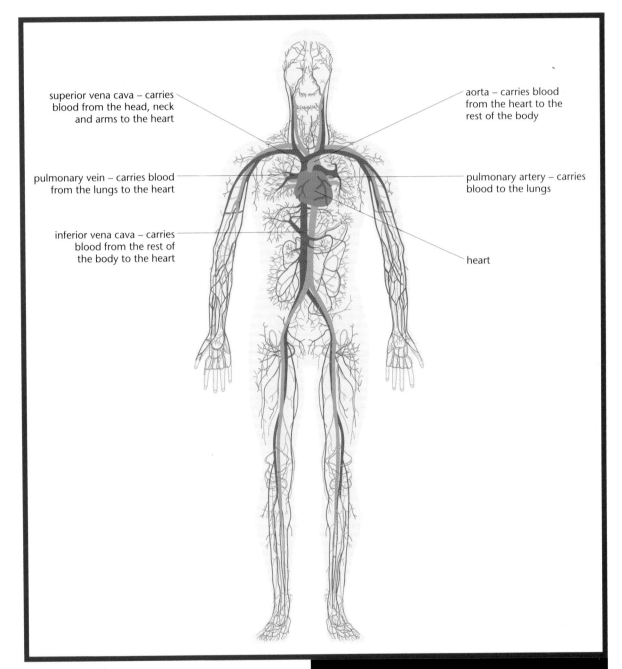

superior vena cava – carries blood from the head, neck and arms to the heart

aorta – carries blood from the heart to the rest of the body

pulmonary vein – carries blood from the lungs to the heart

pulmonary artery – carries blood to the lungs

inferior vena cava – carries blood from the rest of the body to the heart

heart

This diagram shows the position of the heart in the body, and some of the major blood vessels. Arteries are shown in orange and veins are shown in red.

Blood has three main functions:
- transport of oxygen and nutrients to tissues, and removal of carbon dioxide and other waste products
- regulation of levels of water and other chemicals, and maintenance of body temperature
- protection against infection and disease.

To carry out these functions, blood has to travel around the body. Blood travels through a network of tubes called blood vessels. There are three main types – **arteries** (carrying blood away from the heart) **veins** (carrying blood back to the heart) and **capillaries** (linking arteries and veins). These vessels carry the blood to and from every part of the body.

Blood cannot move on its own – it has to be pumped around. The heart is a very strong pump and every time it beats, blood is pumped along the blood vessels.

This is a portrait of William Harvey, who revolutionized 17th-century medicine with his radical ideas about the heart and blood.

Early ideas

Until the 17th century, the works of Galen, an ancient Greek, formed the basis for medical thought. Galen taught that blood was produced by the liver, and used up by the rest of the body. An English doctor, William Harvey, proved this to be wrong. He examined hearts from different animals and studied the flow of blood in the human arm. Harvey was the first person to prove that blood circulates around the body, and that the heart plays an important role in this. His textbook, *On the Motions of the Heart and Blood* was published in 1628, and was a starting point for many other researchers.

THE HEART

An adult, human heart is about the size of a small fist and has a mass of 200–400 grams. It sits almost in the centre of the chest, between the two lungs, and is tipped slightly to the left. It is well-protected by the bones of the ribcage, the sternum (breastbone) and the spine.

Around the heart is a protective layer called the **pericardium**. This contains a liquid (pericardial fluid) that helps to lubricate the heart, allowing it to move freely as it beats. Strong fibres attach the pericardium to the spine and other parts of the chest, keeping the heart firmly in the correct position. Inside the pericardium is the heart wall. This is a thick layer of muscle, with a thin covering of **membrane** on both sides. Like every other muscle in the body, the muscles of the heart need a good supply of blood to bring oxygen and **nutrients**, and take away waste products. The coronary **arteries** bring blood to the heart muscle, and the cardiac **veins** carry blood away from it.

Inside the heart

Inside the heart there are four spaces called chambers. A thick wall, the **septum**, separates the two sides of the heart. Each side has an upper chamber (**atrium**) and a lower chamber (**ventricle**). Blood flows into the heart via the atria (the plural of atrium is atria), and leaves via the

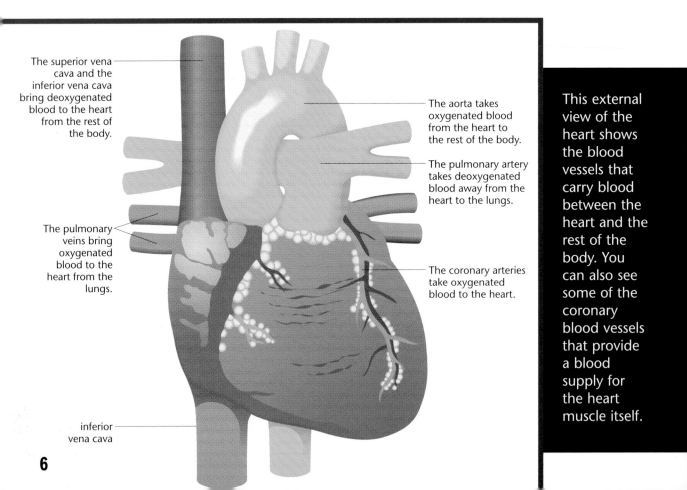

The superior vena cava and the inferior vena cava bring deoxygenated blood to the heart from the rest of the body.

The pulmonary veins bring oxygenated blood to the heart from the lungs.

inferior vena cava

The aorta takes oxygenated blood from the heart to the rest of the body.

The pulmonary artery takes deoxygenated blood away from the heart to the lungs.

The coronary arteries take oxygenated blood to the heart.

This external view of the heart shows the blood vessels that carry blood between the heart and the rest of the body. You can also see some of the coronary blood vessels that provide a blood supply for the heart muscle itself.

6

ventricles. The walls of the atria are thinner than the walls of the ventricles because the atria only have to pump blood into the ventricles, while the ventricles have to work harder to pump blood out of the heart and into the arteries. Blood has to flow through the heart in a one-way system – special flaps called **valves** prevent blood flowing back in the wrong direction. When a valve relaxes, it opens a channel for blood to flow through; when it contracts, it blocks the channel and stops the flow of blood.

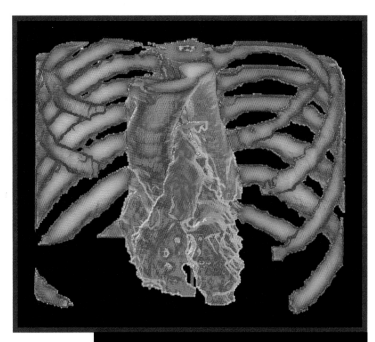

This chest scan shows a healthy human heart (orange, bottom centre) inside the ribcage (pink).

Two separate loops

The heart really acts as two separate pumps, pushing blood around two separate loops:

Lung loop: this is called the **pulmonary circulation**. The right side of the heart pumps blood along the pulmonary arteries to the lungs. In the lungs, blood loses carbon dioxide and collects oxygen. It then travels back to the left side of the heart.

Body loop: this is called the **systemic** circulation. The left side of the heart pumps blood along the **aorta,** and round every part of the body. It takes oxygen to wherever it is needed, and collects and transports nutrients and waste products. It returns to the right side of the heart along two large veins, the inferior vena cava and the superior vena cava. The blood then repeats the lung loop – followed by the body loop – followed by the lung loop … a never-ending cycle.

Heartbeat

Cardiac muscle is able to beat all the time, whether you are awake or asleep. It is called an involuntary muscle – it beats without your ever having to think about it. Under normal conditions, an adult's heart will beat approximately 70 times every minute, with each heartbeat pumping about 70 millilitres of blood – that's more than 100,000 beats every day, 40 million beats in a year!

BLOOD VESSELS

Blood is transported around the body in a network of tubes called blood vessels. Different types of vessels have different structures to allow them to carry out different functions. The main types of blood vessels are **arteries**, **veins** and **capillaries**.

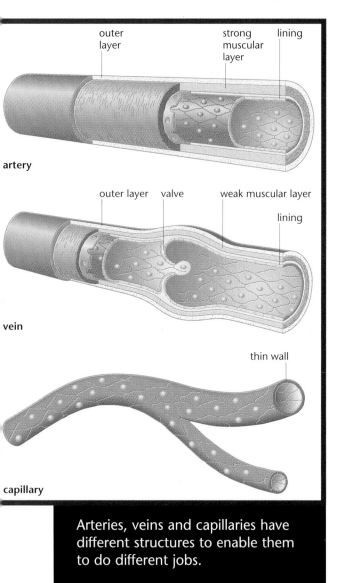

artery

vein

capillary

Arteries, veins and capillaries have different structures to enable them to do different jobs.

Arteries

Arteries carry blood away from the heart to the rest of the body. They have very strong, thick, muscular walls to withstand the high pressure of the blood as it is pumped out of the heart. The diameter of the arteries and the thickness of the walls are greatest in the arteries nearest the heart, as these have to withstand the greatest pressure. The artery wall has three layers:

- a thick outer layer of **collagen** fibres.
- a thick middle layer of elastic and muscle fibres, arranged in rings
- a thin lining layer.

The walls of major arteries are very elastic, allowing them to stretch as the heart pumps blood into them. Blood flows quickly along arteries, in pulses.

Veins

Veins carry blood back to the heart. They have thinner walls than arteries because they carry blood at a lower pressure. Their walls also have three layers:

- a thin outer layer of collagen fibres
- a thin middle layer, containing few muscle fibres
- a thin lining layer.

Blood flows slowly along veins, without a pulse. Veins have a system of **valves**, to prevent blood flowing backwards. When blood is moving towards the heart, the valve is open: blood pushes the flaps of the valve against the inner wall of the vein. If blood begins to flow backwards, it forces the flaps of the valve down, closing the valve and preventing further backflow. Large muscles can also help to keep blood flowing in the right direction in veins – for example, in the lower leg, using the calf muscles squeezes the veins, helping to keep blood flowing back towards the heart.

Blood has to flow from arteries into veins, but it cannot do so directly. Arteries branch and branch again and again, becoming narrower and narrower, eventually forming smaller vessels called **arterioles**. These branch many more times, into the tiniest blood vessels, called capillaries.

Capillaries

Capillaries are very fine, narrow vessels, and they occur in branching networks throughout body tissues. Only a few special tissues, like the cornea and lens of the eye, do not have a capillary network. Capillary walls are made of just a single layer of cells. Gases, **nutrients** and wastes can easily pass through the capillaries from blood into tissues and from tissues into blood by a process called diffusion. This means that particles of a gas or liquid move from an area of high concentration to an area of lower concentration, thus evening out the concentration.

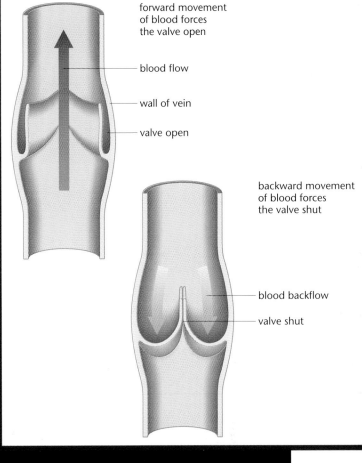

These diagrams show how valves in veins prevent blood flowing backwards. Blood flowing in the right direction pushes the flaps of the valves flat against the wall of the vein. If blood starts to flow backwards, the flaps are pushed down, shutting the valve.

Capillaries unite, forming larger vessels called venules. These unite, forming small veins and eventually large veins.

Exercise

Exercise helps to maintain a healthy **circulation**. The more exercise we do, the faster our heart pumps, and the greater the volume of blood is pumped. Arteries and veins have to cope with this extra workload, and so become stronger and healthier. The heart muscle itself becomes stronger and larger with exercise. A trained athlete's heart can pump more blood, with fewer heartbeats, than the heart of a person who does little exercise. The resting heart rate for an average adult is usually around 70 beats per minute, while that of a trained athlete may be as low as 40–60 beats per minute.

HEART FUNCTION

If you lay your fingers gently on the inside of your wrist, you will feel a gentle, regular beating – your **pulse**. Every time your heart beats, blood is forced along the **arteries**, creating the pulse that you feel. Counting the number of beats in one minute will tell you how quickly your heart is beating. Medical staff use a stethoscope to listen to the actual sounds made by the heart as it beats.

The **atria** and **ventricles** relax and contract in turn. The contraction phase is called systole, and the relaxation phase is called diastole. In a normal heartbeat, the two atria contract (atrial systole), while the two ventricles relax (ventricular diastole). This is followed by the ventricles contracting (ventriculare systole), and the atria relaxing (atrial diastole).

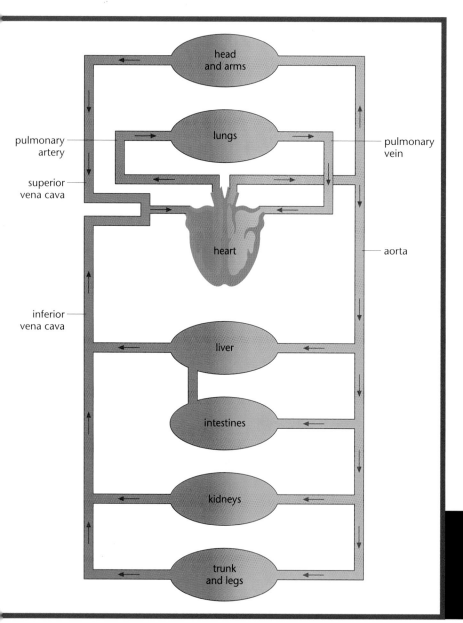

The stages of a heartbeat

The sounds of a heartbeat are made by the **valves** as they shut to control the flow of blood. When you feel your pulse, you feel a single surge of blood, but each heartbeat is made of two separate sounds, one after the other. People often write this as 'lub dup…. lub dup…. lub dup….'

This diagram shows the circulation of the blood to the lungs and to the rest of the body.

These diagrams show the three stages of a heartbeat.

Each heartbeat has three stages:
1 With the valves between the atria and ventricles shut, the atria relax. The right atrium fills with blood from the body and the left atrium fills with blood from the lungs.
2 The blood in the atria pushes against the valves, forcing them open. The atria contract, the ventricles relax and blood flows out of the atria into the ventricles.
3 When the ventricles are full, the pressure of the blood forces the flaps of the lower valves upwards and the valves snap shut. As they shut, they make the first 'lub' sound of the heartbeat. The ventricles then contract, pushing the blood upwards. The upper valves relax and open, allowing blood to flow out of the ventricles into the pulmonary artery and aorta. With the ventricles empty, the upper valves snap shut, creating the second 'dup' sound of the heartbeat.
This is then followed by stage 1 and the start of another heartbeat.

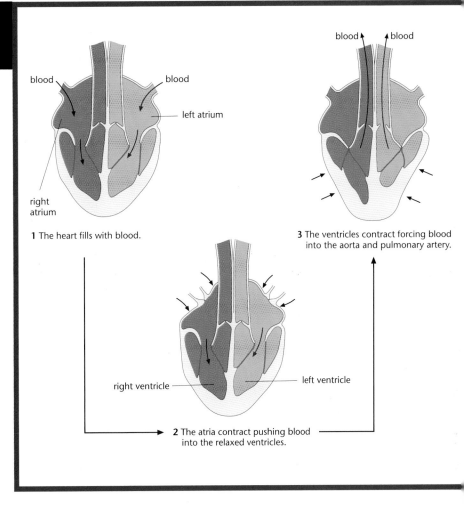

1 The heart fills with blood.

2 The atria contract pushing blood into the relaxed ventricles.

3 The ventricles contract forcing blood into the aorta and pulmonary artery.

Upper and lower valves
The upper and lower valves of the heart operate rather like gates, forced open and shut by the blood pushing against them.
Upper: The valves controlling blood flow from the atria into the ventricles are large and are anchored to the heart wall by strong tendons. As the valves shut, muscles attached to the base of each valve contract to stop them being turned inside out.
Lower: The valves controlling blood flow out of the ventricles are smaller. Each valve has three flaps, attached directly to the heart wall.

HEALTHY HEART

The heart affects every aspect of our lives. It must work efficiently if we are to stay fit and healthy – so it makes sense to take good care of it! Lifestyle – what we do and how we live – has a big effect on the heart and **circulation**. You can do a lot to keep your heart healthy by taking plenty of exercise and eating the right sorts of foods. You should also avoid things such as drinking too much alcohol, smoking cigarettes and taking other drugs.

Aerobic exercises, such as swimming, help to keep the heart healthy and strong.

Exercise is important

Exercise is very important. The heart is a muscle and, like any other muscle, the more it is used the stronger it becomes. Some types of exercise make the heart work harder than others.

Aerobic exercise

Aerobic exercises include activities such as swimming, cycling and running. They all use big body muscles, making big movements, and this increases the amount of oxygen the body needs. To get extra oxygen to the muscles, the heart has to pump blood around the body more quickly. This makes it stronger, and increases the amount of blood that it can pump. These activities can also help to lower the blood pressure, and keep the body weight down. Over a period of time, they can also increase the mass of the heart, making it stronger. Most doctors recommend three to five 20-minute aerobic sessions each week, to keep the heart and circulatory system at peak fitness.

Anaerobic exercise

Anaerobic exercise, like weightlifting and yoga, are good for building up body strength and suppleness. However, because the large body muscles are not repeatedly contracting and relaxing quickly, they are not using much extra oxygen and so the heart does not do much extra work. It is a good idea, for overall fitness, to combine the two types of exercise.

Anaerobic exercise, such as yoga, can help to improve your overall fitness.

Nutrition

The food that we eat is important in keeping the heart and circulatory system in first class condition. The body needs a variety of **nutrients**, so we should try to eat a balanced diet containing meat, fish, eggs or nuts (good sources of **protein**), fruit and vegetables (good sources of **vitamins** and **minerals**), starchy foods (for **carbohydrates**) and dairy products (for proteins and fats). We do need some fats for energy and to provide some chemicals needed for maintaining body tissues, but there is a strong link between eating a lot of fatty foods and developing heart disease. Fat can lead to clogging up of blood vessels, increasing the chance of a heart attack or **stroke**; it can also cause weight gain, and this puts an extra strain on the heart. Some types of fat are better for us than others; good sources of 'healthy fats' include oily fish, such as salmon and sardines, and olive oil.

Polluting the body ...

Polluting the body with alcohol, cigarettes and other drugs is not a very sensible thing to do. All of these have a bad effect on the heart:

- Alcohol can lead to raised blood pressure, and damage to the heart muscle. It also leads to weight gain, making the heart work harder.
- Cigarettes increase the risk of **blood clots**, which can cause strokes and heart attacks. Small blood vessels may become narrower, so the heart is under strain as it works harder to push the blood through.
- Other drugs can have a wide variety of effects on the body. Some, such as cocaine, may have a direct effect on the heart and blood and cause other serious damage to the body, so it is best to avoid them completely. Other drugs, such as caffeine, may have smaller, less serious effects, but it makes sense to limit the amounts that you take in.

HEART ATTACK

The heart muscle needs a constant supply of blood to enable it to function and stay healthy. This is provided by the coronary **arteries**. If the blood flow through these arteries is reduced for any reason, the heart muscle becomes short of oxygen and begins to die: a heart attack.

Causes

The most common cause of a heart attack is blockage of the coronary arteries by a build up of fatty deposits, or by a **blood clot**. This is especially likely in people who have eaten a diet high in fats for many years. A fatty substance can collect on the inside of the artery walls. As more and more builds up, the patches of fatty substance get bigger and bigger. They begin to make the artery narrower, restricting the flow of blood. This can lead to a chest pain called angina.

A blood clot may start to form around these patches. When the blood clot completely blocks a coronary artery, the part of the heart muscle supplied by that artery is starved of blood and dies. This is a severe heart attack.

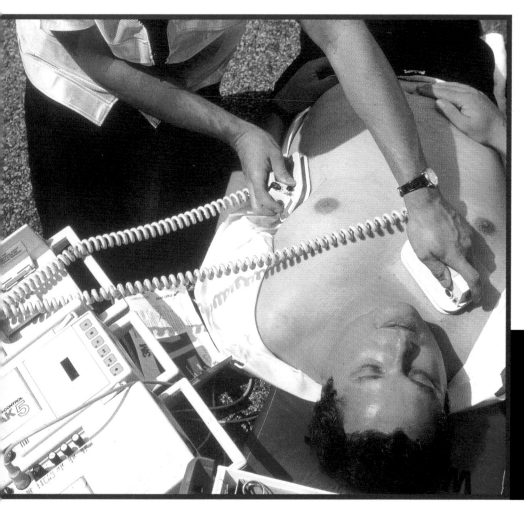

Medical teams can carry out emergency treatment to improve the chances of survival after a heart attack.

Avoiding heart attacks

After suffering a heart attack, many patients are advised to alter their lifestyle. Heart attacks are much more common in people who:

- smoke
- eat a lot of fatty foods
- are overweight
- take little exercise
- suffer a lot of stress.

Patients who have had a heart attack are encouraged to put these things right – and it makes sense for everybody to avoid these things if possible.

Heart attacks can sometimes occur in people who take plenty of exercise, eat healthy diets and do not smoke cigarettes. Some people have a **tendency** to have higher than normal levels of **cholesterol** in their blood, making blocking of arteries more likely. Other diseases, such as diabetes, can also increase the risk of heart attacks. There may be **genetic** links too, as some families do seem to be more at risk of heart disease than others.

Symptoms

The main symptom of a heart attack is serious chest pain, often accompanied by pain or tingling in the left arm. A patient may also be sweating, feel sick and find it hard to breathe.

It is important to get medical help to a heart attack patient as quickly as possible. The medical team will be able to assess the situation, and give the patient drugs to relieve the pain. If the patient is unconscious, has stopped breathing and has no **pulse**, they may give mouth to mouth resuscitation and heart massage, to try to maintain an oxygen supply and keep the blood **circulating**. The heart muscles may simply twitch (fibrillate) instead of contracting properly; defibrillation equipment can be used to give an electric shock, to stimulate the heart to begin beating again. Drugs can be given to dissolve the clot, and to reduce the chances of another clot forming.

Treatment

A patient who has suffered a heart attack is likely to spend some time in hospital, where they can rest and be monitored. Some patients may need an operation to re-route some blood vessels to improve the blood supply to the heart. When doctors feel that they are well enough, patients need to slowly build up their level of activity again. A range of drugs, including aspirin, may need to be taken for a long time after a heart attack to reduce the risks of future heart attacks occurring.

HEART MONITORING

For most hospital patients, counting the **pulse** is a routine procedure. For patients with heart problems, monitoring and investigating the heartbeat can help medical staff to assess how well the heart is functioning and decide on the best form of treatment.

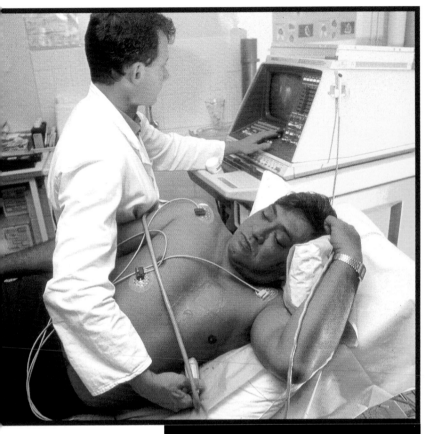

This patient's heart function is being investigated using an ultrasound echocardiogram.

Listening to the heart

Using a stethoscope, a doctor can listen to the sounds made by the heart as the **valves** open and shut and the blood flows through. Unusual rushing or gurgling noises may indicate that one or more valves are not working properly, and the doctor may decide to send the patient for further investigations. Conditions such as heart murmurs may be monitored regularly, to check that the heart function is stable.

Ultrasound echocardiogram

Heart function can be monitored using an ultrasound echocardiogram. This machine sends high-frequency sound waves through the chest. The waves bounce off the heart and are converted into electrical signals that can be displayed on a monitor. All four chambers of the heart and the valves can be seen. Echocardiograms can be used to detect **blood clots**, faulty valves, tumours and other problems.

Electrocardiograph

Another method for investigating the heart is to use an electrocardiograph (ECG). As the heart beats, the muscle creates electrical changes. Electrodes that can detect these changes are attached to the patient's chest, arms and legs and the results are displayed on a monitor or a chart recorder. Information from an ECG can confirm whether or not a patient has suffered a heart attack. It can also be used to detect whether any areas of the heart are damaged.

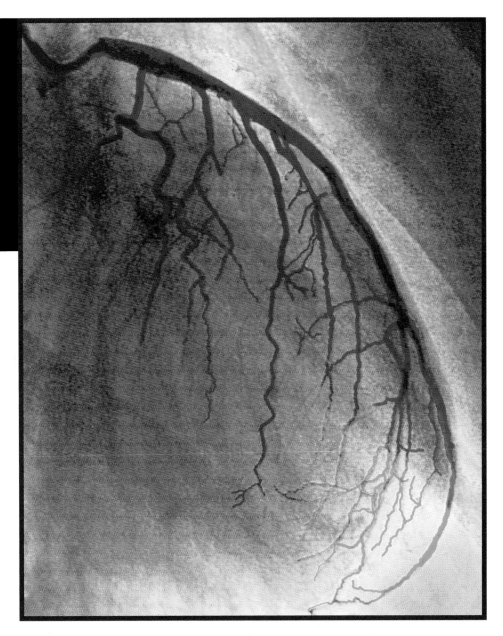

This view of the coronary blood vessels (pink/blue) that feed the heart (red) was made after a patient was injected with a chemical that shows up on an X-ray.

Nuclear scanning

If a radioactive chemical, such as technetium or thallium, is injected into the bloodstream, it will be carried to every part of the body. Using a special camera that detects radioactivity, a nuclear scanner can create a colour-coded picture of the heart as it beats. This can show the blood passing through the heart, dead or damaged heart muscle, and areas of the heart that are short of oxygen.

Angiocardiography

Angiocardiography is another way of looking inside the heart. A hollow, flexible tube is inserted into a **vein** in the thigh, arm or neck and moved slowly along until it reaches the heart. Dyes can be injected via the tube and then detected by a special camera and displayed on a monitor.

HEART SURGERY

In adults, surgery can improve heart function and reduce the risks of future heart attacks. Some babies are born with heart **defects**, and these may need immediate surgery to keep the baby alive. Other less serious conditions can be corrected when the child is a little older. Surgical techniques are improving and advancing all the time; one of the greatest breakthroughs in heart surgery was the invention of the heart lung machine.

Heart lung machine

It is very difficult to operate on a heart that is beating and full of blood. Ideally, the heart should be still and empty – but blood must collect oxygen and circulate to all parts of the body if the patient is to survive. In 1953, the first heart lung machine was introduced. Blood flowed from the venae cavae through a pump to an oxygenator, where waste carbon dioxide was removed and oxygen, which is needed by all the body organs and tissues, was added – as in the lungs. The blood then passed through a filter and was pumped back into the **aorta**, and around the rest of the body. For the first time, a patient could be kept alive without their own heart working. This meant that heart surgeons could attempt far more complex surgery than ever before.

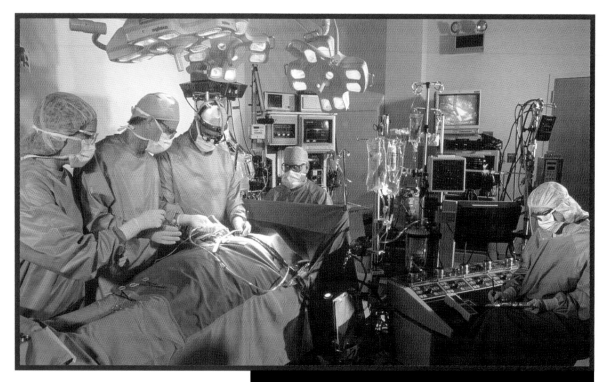

The heart lung machine takes over the function of the heart and lungs during heart surgery. Blood is pumped from the venae cavae, through the oxygenator and filter, then back to the body.

Heart lung machines have been refined and developed since the first one was introduced. The patient's body is often cooled so that there is no heart movement at all; the very newest methods allow doctors to cool just the heart and not the rest of the body.

Coronary artery bypass

In patients who have narrowed, blocked or damaged coronary **arteries**, the blood supply to the heart is restricted and the heart is unable to function properly. This means that the patient is less and less able to carry on with normal everyday activities; even small tasks can cause breathlessness and the severe pain of angina. An operation to bypass a section of the coronary artery – a coronary artery bypass – may help such patients. A blood vessel is taken from another part of the body and **grafted** to a coronary artery, either side of a blockage. The blood can then flow along the new vessel, bypassing the blockage. The blood supply to the heart muscle is improved, allowing the patient greater mobility and levels of activity than before.

Angioplasty

If coronary arteries are blocked, the blood supply to the heart muscle becomes reduced. Angioplasty is a method of unblocking the coronary arteries. A plastic tube is put into an artery, often in the groin, and guided to the coronary vessels. Dye inserted into the tube is carried to the coronary vessels, and blockages can be seen on angiograms (X-rays of blood vessels). A tiny air-filled balloon can then be inserted, via the tube, to squash the blockage back against the blood vessel wall. This allows blood to flow again. A coil of stainless steel, called a stent, can also be inserted via the tube to hold the vessel open permanently.

Heart surgery in babies

Most babies are born with normal, healthy hearts, but some have defects that require heart surgery. If a baby is born with a hole in the wall between the two sides of the heart, blood can move freely from one side of the heart to the other. This means that the **oxygenated** blood does not get pumped round properly to the rest of the body. A surgeon can close the hole either by stitching it, or by putting a plastic patch over it. Blood can then circulate normally, and the baby will be fit and healthy.

Blood vessels carrying blood to and from the heart may be incorrectly connected to the heart, or may be narrow or badly formed. Surgery to connect the heart and vessels correctly can be carried out, vessels can be mended and narrow vessels can be widened to improve blood flow.

PACEMAKERS

The heart must beat regularly for blood to be **circulated** efficiently around the body. Normally, it is stimulated to do this by its own pacemaker. The heart's natural pacemaker is the sinoatrial node (SA node), a small, specialized area of the right **atrium**. It generates an electrical signal about 70 times every minute when the body is resting. This stimulates the heart muscle, making the atria and then the **ventricles** contract, pumping blood out of the heart. If this does not function properly, an artificial pacemaker can be implanted into the patient to take over the regulation of the heartbeat.

Arrhythmia

A normal heartbeat can be disrupted if the SA node develops an abnormal rhythm or rate, if the normal pathway for the electrical signal is interrupted, or if another part of the heart takes over as pacemaker. The electrical signals may be erratic: too fast, too slow, or too irregular.

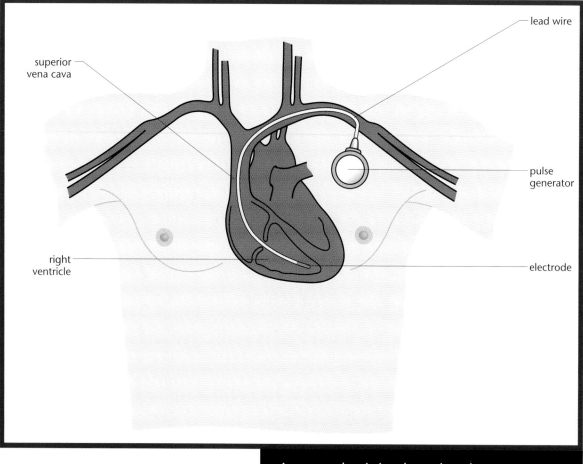

superior vena cava

right ventricle

lead wire

pulse generator

electrode

A pacemaker is implanted under the skin, close to the collarbone.

The erratic heartbeat that results is called an 'arrhythmia'. An arrhythmia can mean that the body does not receive enough blood. The patient may feel weak and tired, dizzy and faint; the blood pressure may drop and they may feel heart palpitations (rapid or irregular heartbeats).

Artificial pacemakers

Artificial pacemakers take over the task of regulating the heartbeat. Arrhythmias can affect people of all ages – tiny babies, young children, teenagers and adults; artificial pacemakers can be used whatever the age of the patient. There are several different types of device that can do this, but they all work on the same basic principles.

A permanent pacemaker is implanted under the skin, usually just below the collarbone. Some simply send electrical signals to start or regulate a slow heartbeat. Others can also monitor the heartbeat, and only send signals if it becomes slow or irregular. Some modern pacemakers can also adjust the rate of heartbeat, increasing the rate when the patient is undertaking some physical activity. Pacemakers can send signals to a single chamber of the heart; more sophisticated pacemakers can be used if two chambers need to be regulated. There are a variety of different designs of pacemakers, all slightly different shapes and sizes.

Battery power

Pacemakers are run by a special battery that generates timed electrical signals. Like all batteries, the battery of a pacemaker does not last for ever, so although they usually last a few years, they do need to be replaced eventually. This can be done under **local anaesthetic**. They also need to be checked regularly to ensure that they are working properly, and that the battery does not need to be changed. Modern pacemakers can be tested and adjusted painlessly from outside the body using a radio-wave programmer.

Living with a pacemaker

A pacemaker can help a patient with an arrhythmia lead a normal, active life, doing things like driving, swimming, sports and other activities. Most medicines do not affect pacemakers, and neither do electrical tools and equipment such as televisions and microwaves. However, pacemakers can trigger security devices at airports! This can be embarrassing for the patient – but it will not damage the pacemaker, or stop it working properly.

The four **valves** of the heart control the flow of blood. If these are damaged or do not function properly, blood may not be pumped efficiently to the rest of the body. Babies may be born with faulty valves. Valves may be damaged by diseases such as rheumatic fever and **bacterial infections**. Ageing and normal wear and tear may weaken or stiffen heart valves. To restore efficient blood **circulation**, faulty valves may require surgical repair or replacement.

Heart murmur

Heart valve defects can often be detected using a stethoscope. The normal lub ... dup sounds of the heartbeat may be hidden by the sounds of blood rushing through the heart. This is called a heart murmur, and it usually indicates a valve disorder. A heart murmur may be caused by:

- backflow of blood through a valve that does not close properly. The heart works less efficiently because it has to pump some blood twice. The heart chambers may also be enlarged because they have to hold more blood.
- restricted blood flow because a valve does not open properly. Blood pressure in the heart increases because blood builds up behind the faulty valve. The heart has to work harder to pump the higher-pressure blood.

If the damage to a valve is not too severe, a surgeon may be able to repair it. Stretched tissue can be removed, and the edges may be stitched together.

Using animal valves

There is a lot of debate about whether it is right to use animals to cure humans. Some people argue that it is perfectly justifiable to kill a pig and remove the heart valves if this will save a person's life, and allow them to live normally and be active. Other people argue that we should respect animals and we have no right to use them in this way. What do you think? Would you want to have a pig's valve if you were ill? Or would you risk dying rather than hurt an animal? The debate will go on and on ...

Replacement valves

A valve that is seriously damaged may need to be replaced with a new one. Several types of valve are available:

- from human donors: valves from a donated human heart are frozen in liquid nitrogen until the day before the operation. Very delicate surgery is needed to ensure that the donor valves fit the patient's heart exactly.
- from human tissue: a new valve can be constructed using tissue, such as part of the vena cava, from the patient's own body. The tissue is attached to a stainless steel frame to strengthen it, and is then inserted into the heart.
- from animals: valves from pigs' hearts can be successfully inserted into human hearts. Tissue from cows' hearts can also be used to make replacement valves for human hearts.
- artificial valves: a lot of research has been carried out to design and produce an artificial heart valve. The first, made in 1952, was a ball valve. The ball was pushed up, opening the valve, when blood was pumped out of the heart chamber. When blood flowed backwards, it pushed the ball back into place, closing the valve. Single disk valves were introduced in 1965, and the design was refined and improved to produce the first bi-leaflet valve in 1977. These have two disks and a hinge, and have proved to be very successful. Patients are living longer, and having fewer complications, than with the original ball valves.

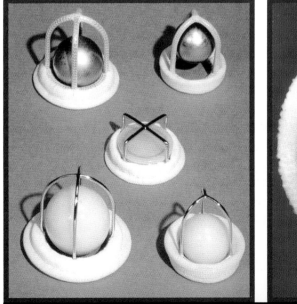 

(left) A selection of ball valves: as blood is pumped out of the heart chamber, it lifts the ball; backflow of blood pushes the ball back into place. (right) A modern bi-leaflet valve, with two disks and a hinge.

HEART TRANSPLANT

For some patients, heart disease may be too serious for surgical repair. For many years, doctors could do little to help, and the patients would eventually die. The first successful human heart transplant offered a way of treating these patients, giving them a chance of life.

Rejection

The main problem that the early heart transplant patients faced was rejection: their **immune system** recognized the donor heart as 'foreign', and attacked it in the same way as it would attack an infection. Drugs were developed to suppress the immune system and overcome the rejection problem. Although these were largely successful, they led to an increased risk of infection and other illnesses; without an active immune system, infections that are normally relatively minor can rapidly become very serious.

Stages of a transplant

The main stages of a heart transplant are:

Finding a suitable donor: tissue typing tries to match the donor's cells as closely as possible to the patient's, to reduce the risk of rejection.

Transporting the donor heart: the donor and patient are rarely at the same hospital, and the operation has to take place as quickly as possible after the donor's death. The donor heart is packed into sterile bags, stored at 4°C and transported by aeroplane or helicopter; land transport usually has a police escort to ensure maximum speed.

Preparation for surgery: while the donor heart is being transported, the operation on the patient begins. The chest is opened, and everything is made ready for the new heart to arrive.

The transplant: the patient's blood **circulation** is maintained by a heart lung machine. The new heart is put into place, and the blood vessels are connected. It usually begins to beat straight away.

After the transplant: the patient is usually conscious within a few hours. Immunosuppressive drugs are taken to prevent rejection of the new heart, and strict precautions are followed to prevent infection.

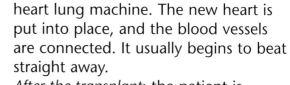

Dr. Christian Barnard, the surgeon who carried out the first heart transplant, is on the left in this picture.

The first transplants

For many years, doctors had been experimenting with transplanting tissues and organs. The first successful human heart transplant was carried out on 3 December, 1967, by Dr Christian Barnard in Cape Town, South Africa. The patient was Louis Washkansky, a 55 year-old grocer. The heart he received came from a 24 year-old woman who had been killed in a car crash.

Louis Washkansky only lived for 18 days after his transplant operation; this may not seem very long, but it was enough to prove to doctors around the world that transplants could be successfully carried out. In January 1968, a second transplant was carried out; the patient, Philip Blaiberg, lived for 563 days afterwards.

Artificial hearts

Because heart transplants are very expensive, and there is a shortage of donor hearts, operations are only carried out on patients who are very seriously ill with severe heart disease. Without a transplant, these patients would die. Researchers have worked for years to design an artificial heart, but it has proved difficult to produce one that is reliable and safe. In July 2001, a major advance was made when an artificial heart was successfully implanted into a patient, Robert Tools, at a hospital in Louisville, USA. The device, which weighs about 900 grams, is made of titanium and a special plastic. It has an internal battery that lasts for about half an hour, long enough for a patient to take a shower or other brief activity; an external battery pack has to be worn at all other times, to keep the device pumping blood around the body. This is a very positive and encouraging breakthrough, and an identical device has since been implanted into a second patient. If they are found to be successful in the long term, these artificial hearts could benefit many patients suffering from heart disease.

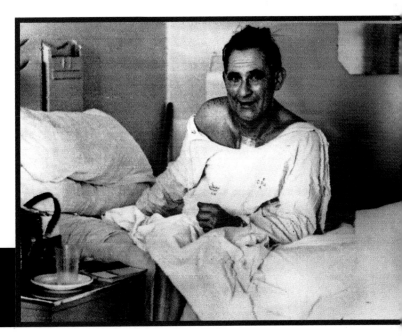

Louis Washkansky is seen here sitting up in bed after having the first successful heart transplant.

PROBLEMS WITH ARTERIES

Arteries are the vessels that carry blood, rich in oxygen, to all parts of the body. If they become blocked or damaged, the blood supply is interrupted, causing a variety of problems.

Atherosclerosis

Atherosclerosis occurs when fat, **fibrin** and other debris collects on the inside of an artery wall. Eating a lot of fatty foods, smoking cigarettes and being very overweight can all increase the risk of this occurring. The lining of a healthy artery is pale and smooth. An unhealthy artery has yellow streaks, and a roughened surface. Thick white fibres are formed, making irregular bumps that restrict the blood flow. As the blood flows over these lumps, some blood cells stick to the rough surface, and a **blood clot** (a thrombus) may form.

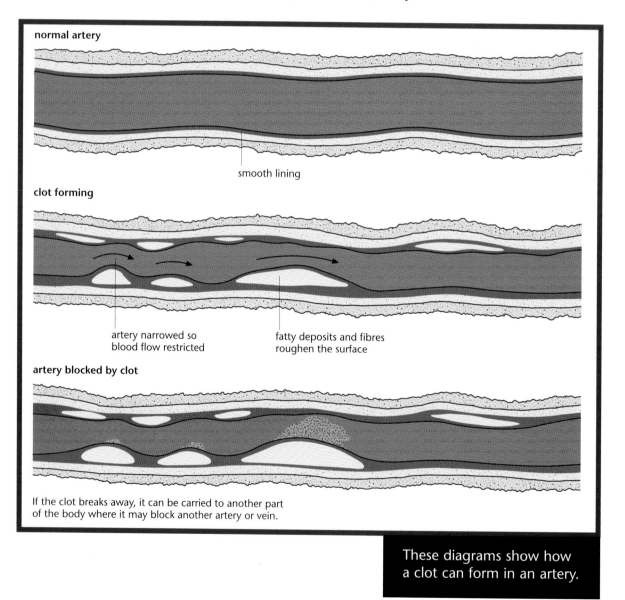

normal artery

smooth lining

clot forming

artery narrowed so
blood flow restricted

fatty deposits and fibres
roughen the surface

artery blocked by clot

If the clot breaks away, it can be carried to another part
of the body where it may block another artery or vein.

These diagrams show how
a clot can form in an artery.

Thrombosis

A blood clot may block an artery, stopping blood flow. This is called a thrombosis. If a blood clot blocks a coronary artery, a heart attack may follow. If it blocks an artery supplying blood to the brain, the patient may suffer a **stroke**. The brain needs a continuous supply of oxygen and if this is interrupted for even a short time there may be temporary or permanent brain damage, and it may even be fatal. An angiogram can show exactly where the blockage is, and drugs may be injected to dissolve the clot.

Embolism

If a blood clot breaks free from the damaged artery, it may travel around the body in the blood stream and cause a blockage (an embolism) in an artery somewhere else. Blocked arteries can sometimes be cleared by injection of a drug to dissolve the blood clot. If an embolism blocks an artery taking blood to the brain, the patient may suffer a stroke.

Aneurism

Atherosclerosis can make an artery wall weak, causing a section of it to stretch and bulge like a balloon. This is called an aneurism. Although the bulge itself may not cause a problem, because it is weakened it may burst at any time. This causes internal bleeding (haemorrhage), and the patient is likely to suffer severe pain and shock. If the aneurism is in an artery supplying blood to the brain, it may cause a stroke.

Raynaud's disease

Capillaries in the skin can help to regulate body temperature. When the body gets hot, **arterioles** force more blood into the capillaries. As the blood passes close to the surface of the skin, it loses heat and the body cools down. When the body gets cold, arterioles restrict the amount of blood flowing into the capillaries. Less blood flows to the surface of the skin, and heat is conserved. Raynaud's disease causes the arterioles in the fingers and toes to constrict, reducing blood supply to capillaries, sometimes just for a few minutes, sometimes for much longer. The fingers and toes turn white and cold. When the arterioles relax, blood rushes back into the capillaries, causing intense pain and tingling. Raynaud's disease is much worse in cold weather as the tiny blood capillaries constrict, and almost completely stop blood flow to the affected areas. Sufferers try to avoid the pain by keeping hands and feet well wrapped up in warm gloves and socks.

Veins carry **deoxygenated** blood back to the heart. As it travels around the body, the blood collects waste carbon dioxide produced by the organs and tissues. Any problems with veins may lead to reduced efficiency of blood **circulation**, causing problems in other organs and tissues.

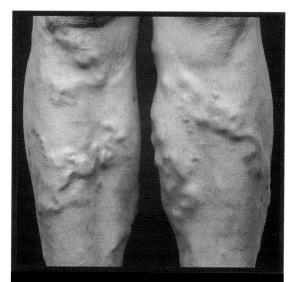

Varicose veins most commonly affect the legs of elderly women. In severe cases, like this, surgery might be needed.

Varicose veins

Varicose veins occur most often in the legs. If the **valves** become weak, blood flows backwards and collects in pools. This stretches the veins, and eventually they become permanently stretched and twisted. They may be seen as dark, knotty threads under the skin.

Often, they cause little problem and no treatment is needed. Mild symptoms can include swelling in the lower legs, pain and cramps; these can often be eased by wearing elastic stockings which squeeze inwards on the leg preventing swelling. More serious cases can be treated by injections of drugs, and others may need surgery.

Varicose veins may be due to a **hereditary** valve weakness, but can also be made worse by pregnancy, lack of exercise and smoking. People whose jobs require them to stand for a long time often develop varicose veins.

Phlebitis

Phlebitis is inflammation of a vein, usually the result of an injury or infection. It occurs most often in the veins of the legs. The area may be swollen, the leg may feel heavy and uncomfortable and a red streak may appear along the line of the vein.

Phlebitis is usually treated by resting with the legs raised, painkillers, and **antibiotics** if there is an infection; elastic stockings and bandages may help to reduce the swelling.

Deep Vein Thrombosis (DVT)

When a **blood clot** (thrombus) develops in a deep vein, usually in the thigh or calf, the blood flow through the vein is restricted or stopped

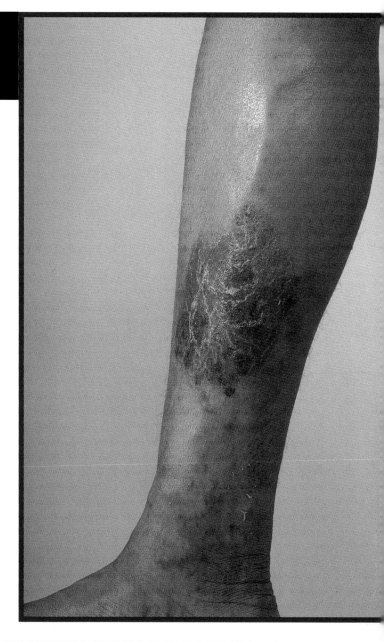

Blood is not flowing properly through the veins of this leg, causing the skin to be discoloured and flaky.

completely. DVT can occur when circulation is poor, due to heart disease, severe varicose veins, or lack of exercise.

DVT can cause tenderness or a sharp pain in the leg, fever and a rapid heartbeat. If a clot breaks free, it can travel to other parts of the body, the most common being the lungs. If it blocks an **artery** in the lungs it can cause a **pulmonary embolism**, which can be fatal. Tests for DVT include an ultrasound scan, X-rays of the veins after injection of dye and tests to find out how quickly your blood clots. Treatment usually includes anti-coagulant drugs that make the blood less 'sticky' and therefore prevent more clots forming. Patients can also help to prevent clots forming by avoiding knee socks that restrict blood flow, resting with feet raised, wearing elasticated stockings and keeping toes and ankles moving regularly.

Economy class syndrome

DVT has been found to occur more frequently in people who have had long airline flights. It is thought that because they have little legroom, passengers do not move around enough to keep blood flowing efficiently. The media often call this 'economy class syndrome' because space is more restricted in cheaper airline seats, making it harder to move around. Although it can affect anybody, people most likely to suffer DVT during a flight are those who are overweight, pregnant, elderly, smokers or already suffering from heart disease. Doctors suggest that you can reduce the risk of DVT during a flight by wriggling your toes and bending your ankles regularly, and walking up and down the aisle at least once an hour.

BLOOD PRESSURE

When the **ventricles** of the heart contract, blood is pumped into the **arteries**. The force with which it is pushed against the walls of the arteries is called the 'blood pressure'. Doctors measure blood pressure using a sphygmomanometer and a stethoscope. High blood pressure can increase the risk of some other illnesses.

Blood pressure depends on four things:
- the volume of blood in the arteries
- the elasticity of the artery walls
- the rate at which the ventricles contract
- the force with which the ventricles contract.

Systolic pressure is the highest pressure inside the arteries; it occurs when the ventricles contract. Diastolic pressure is the lowest pressure inside the arteries; it occurs when the ventricles are relaxed, just before they contract again.

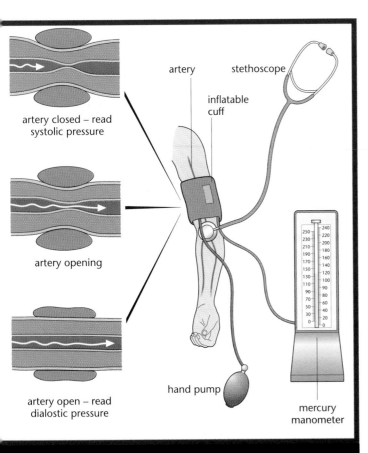

artery closed – read systolic pressure

artery opening

artery open – read dialostic pressure

artery

stethoscope

inflatable cuff

hand pump

mercury manometer

In this diagram, you can see what happens when blood pressure is measured. Pressure from the cuff completely closes the artery in the top diagram. The artery is partially open in the middle diagram and fully open in the bottom one.

Measuring blood pressure

A cuff is wrapped around the patient's arm and inflated as the doctor squeezes a rubber bulb. As the cuff is inflated, it squeezes the arm and squashes the main artery on the inside of the arm shut, cutting off the blood flow. The doctor places the stethoscope over the route of the artery and listens. When the pressure is just above systolic pressure, the artery is closed completely and there will be no sounds through the stethoscope. The doctor can read the pressure off the scale of the sphygmomanometer. The cuff is then allowed to deflate slowly and as the artery begins to open, the doctor will hear sounds of blood rushing through the artery. The sounds get louder and then quieter again as the blood flow returns to normal. When the sounds stop completely, blood is flowing normally and the diastolic pressure can be read from the scale.

In this photograph, the girl's blood pressure is being measured by her doctor.

Blood pressure is measured in millimetres of mercury (mmHg) – the amount of pressure needed to raise the mercury in the sphygmomanometer scale. A normal, healthy young adult would expect to have a systolic pressure of 120mmHg and a diastolic pressure of 80mmHg. This is written as 120/80mmHg.

Blood pressure changes with age. A newborn baby's blood pressure is very low and it gradually increases during the first few months of life. As we age, blood pressure often increases. It is considered to be high if it is greater than 140/90 mmHg.

Hypertension

High blood pressure is also called hypertension. The arterial walls may be hard and thick, and less elastic than usual, making the heart work harder to pump blood.

There are usually no symptoms of high blood pressure and it is often only detected when a patient goes to a doctor with some unrelated problem. It becomes more common as people get older and is linked to obesity, stress, a high-fat diet, smoking and lack of exercise. Drugs can often be prescribed to reduce blood pressure, but the best treatment is a change of lifestyle – losing weight, improving the diet, giving up smoking and increasing exercise can all have a beneficial effect on blood pressure.

BLOOD

Blood is a liquid containing millions of red blood cells that make it look red. It also contains millions of white blood cells. Blood has three main functions – transport, regulation and protection. It transports oxygen and carbon dioxide, **nutrients** and waste products, **hormones**, drugs and heat. Blood helps to regulate pH levels, preventing body fluids from becoming too acidic or too alkaline; it also helps to regulate body temperature and the water content of tissues. Blood clots to prevent excess blood loss after injury and it also provides defence against infection and disease.

Temperature control

The blood maintains body temperature. The temperature of the blood is raised as it passes through the liver and muscles. The heat is then carried to all tissues as the blood flows through them. To lose heat, capillaries in the skin dilate (relax), allowing more blood to flow through and therefore increasing heat loss. To retain heat, blood capillaries in the skin constrict (narrow), reducing the amount of blood that flows through and therefore reducing heat loss.

Plasma

The liquid part of the blood is called **plasma**. It is about 92 per cent water and 8 per cent **solutes**, mainly plasma **proteins**. All nutrients, waste products, hormones and drugs dissolve in the plasma and are transported around the body. Water is also transported as part of the plasma. Water moves between body tissues and blood plasma by osmosis, a process similar to diffusion, to maintain the water content of body tissues and fluids.

In addition to the plasma, there are three main elements of the blood: red blood cells, white blood cells and **platelets**.

Red blood cells

Red blood cells (erythrocytes) are disc-shaped, with concave top and bottom surfaces, about 0.007–0.008 millimetres in diameter. Their shape allows them to squeeze through narrow capillaries without being damaged. They are simple fluid-filled sacs, each containing about 280 million **molecules** of **haemoglobin**, the **protein** that gives blood its red colour and carries oxygen. Red blood cells are made in **bone marrow** and live for about 120 days. At the end of this time they become fragile and begin to lose their shape. They are then broken down by the **spleen** and the liver.

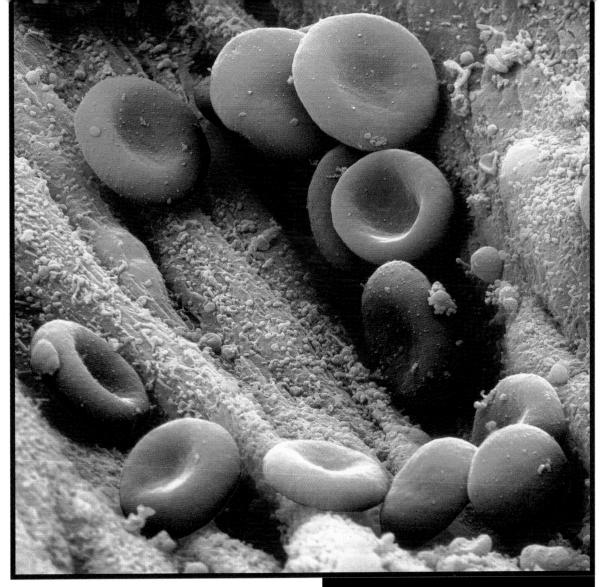

The hollowed-out disc shape of red blood cells allows them to squeeze through capillaries without damage.

White blood cells

White blood cells come in a variety of shapes and sizes, and play important roles in protecting the body against infection and disease. They all have nuclei and some also contain large granules. Some granules contain **enzymes** that can help to destroy foreign material such as **bacteria** and **virus** particles. Some cells surround foreign material and destroy it, and some develop a 'memory' of foreign material so that a swift defence can be mounted if the material is met again. Others kill bacteria and infectious agents.

Platelets

Platelets are disc-shaped cell fragments 0.002–0.004 millimetres in diameter. They stop blood loss from cuts by forming platelet 'plugs', and their granules contain chemicals that make the blood clot.

BLOOD GROUPS AND BLOOD TRANSFUSIONS

The surfaces of red blood cells are made up from many different **molecules**. Blood can be put into different groups depending on which molecules are present or absent. Blood grouping is important when giving **blood transfusions** and organ transplants, as red blood cells from different groups may stick together if they are mixed.

The major blood groups

The major blood grouping system is known as ABO. It was discovered in 1900 by an Austrian doctor, Karl Landsteiner. Two of the different molecules that act as antigens (chemicals which can cause a response by blood cells) may be found on the surfaces of red blood cells: antigen A and antigen B. A person's blood group depends on which of these two antigens are present on their red blood cells. The blood **plasma** also contains chemicals called antibodies, which can bind to antigens on the red blood cells. A person's plasma only contains antibodies to antigens that are not on their own blood cells.

Blood group	Antigen present on red blood cells	Antibody present in plasma
A	A	anti-B
B	B	anti-A
AB	A and B	none
O	neither A nor B	anti-A and anti-B

Mixing blood groups

If group A blood is mixed with group B blood, the plasma antibodies will bind to the red blood cells, making them stick together and form clumps (agglutinate). If this happened in the body, the clumps would prevent blood **circulating** properly. The red blood cells may also become damaged and burst. It is therefore very important to match donor and recipient blood for a blood transfusion. Group O people can donate blood to people with any of the other blood groups because there are no antigens on the group O red blood cells to trigger agglutination. Group AB people can receive blood from any of the other blood groups – they already have both A and B antigens so there will be nothing new to trigger agglutination.

The Rhesus system

Another major blood grouping system is the Rhesus system. It gets its name because the Rhesus factor was first identified in Rhesus

Before the Rhesus factor was discovered in Rhesus monkeys, blood transfusions were a risky procedure.

monkeys. An antigen called Rhesus factor may be present on the surface of red blood cells. If you have Rhesus factor on your red blood cells, you are Rhesus positive (Rh+). If your red blood cells do not have Rhesus factor you are Rhesus negative (Rh-). If an Rh- person is given Rh+ blood, they will make antibodies against Rhesus factor and destroy the red blood cells. It is therefore important to match Rh groups for blood transfusion.

If an Rh- woman has a baby with an Rh+ man, their baby may also be Rh+. The mother's blood will mix with the baby's blood when her baby is born, and the mother will make anti-Rh antibodies. These will not harm the first baby, but if she has a second Rh+ baby the antibodies in her blood will destroy the baby's red blood cells. Until recent years, these babies needed an immediate blood transfusion at birth to save their lives. Now, the mother can be given an injection as soon as her first baby is born to prevent her making the antibodies, therefore protecting any future Rh+ babies she may have.

The ABO and Rhesus systems are the most important blood grouping systems, but many more have been identified. They are not important in blood transfusions, but when patients receive organ transplants they are matched as closely as possible. They are also potentially useful when deciding whether a man is a child's father or not because the blood groups are all inherited from our parents.

Blood is collected from donors, and screened carefully to make sure it is free from disease. **Blood transfusions** are needed when patients undergo major surgery or when there is blood loss after an accident. Other patients may need just some components of blood, such as red blood cells or **plasma**.

Before a person gives blood, they are asked questions about their health, age, weight and recent travel to other countries. Their blood is also checked to make sure that they are not **anaemic**. The donor sits or lies down, and the inside of their elbow is cleaned. A new, sterile needle is inserted into the **vein**. The other end of the needle is attached to a plastic tube leading to a collecting bag. As the donor squeezes his or her hand, blood flows from the vein down the tube and into the collecting bag. Usually one unit of blood (one pint – just over half a litre) is collected. The donor is then given some refreshments such as tea and biscuits, and allowed to rest.

Most people feel fine after donating blood; the body replaces the fluid lost within about 24 hours and the red blood cells are replaced within a few weeks.

After collection, the blood is sent to a laboratory for testing. ABO and Rh groups are tested, and the blood is screened to make sure that it is free from potentially dangerous diseases, such as hepatitis, HIV and syphilis.

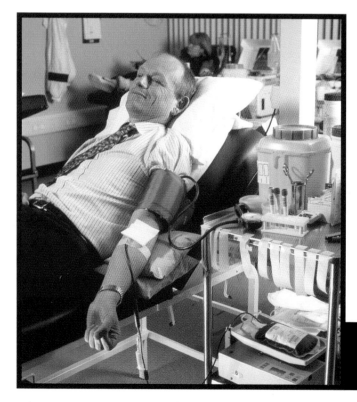

Separation of the blood

Blood can be transfused as whole blood, but as many patients only need some of its components, it makes sense to separate them so that several patients can benefit from one unit of blood. It is usually separated into:

- Red blood cells: these can be stored in a refrigerator for several weeks, or can be frozen for years. They can be used for treating anaemia.

It takes about 20 minutes to donate one unit of blood.

Where and who?

When a person donates blood, they visit a blood donation centre. This may be at a hospital, or a special building. Others are mobile units that travel to different places to make sure that they are accessible to as many people as possible. Some large companies allow them to visit their sites, encouraging employees to donate, and in some countries, mobile units visit schools, colleges, churches and community organizations.

Regulations differ from country to country, but most have a minimum age below which you are not allowed to donate blood; in the UK you must be between 18 and 60 to donate for the first time, while in the USA you must be at least 17 – and there is no upper age limit.

- **Platelets**: are stored at room temperature for a few days only. They are used for treating leukaemia and other conditions where there is a platelet deficiency.
- Plasma: can be stored frozen for several years. It can be used to control bleeding as it contains special chemicals that will help blood to clot.
- White blood cells: must be used within 24 hours of collection. Doctors are still experimenting to find out how useful they may be to help fight infections.

Other products that can be made from blood include clotting factors that play an essential part in controlling **haemophilia**.

This table shows how the incidence of blood groups differs between population groups in the USA.

Unfortunately, there always seems to be a shortage of blood – people are always going to be ill, and there will always be accidents. It is up to everybody to make sure that the blood banks are full – after all, you never know when you might need it yourself!

Population Group	Blood Group (percentage)				
	O	A	B	AB	Rh+
White	45	40	11	4	85
Black	49	27	20	4	95
Korean	32	28	30	10	100
Japanese	31	38	21	10	100
Chinese	42	27	25	6	100
Native American	79	16	4	1	100

Haemophilia is an inherited disease that affects the ability of the blood to clot – the blood clots slowly, or not at all. Because of the way it is inherited, it nearly always affects men and not women. People with haemophilia bruise very easily and badly, and even a tiny scratch can be dangerous, as the bleeding is difficult to stop.

Blood clotting

Blood clotting happens as the result of a chain reaction involving a series of chemical reactions. Each step in the chain triggers the next one. The chain starts with Factor 12, which triggers Factor 11; Factor 11 triggers Factor 10 … and so it goes on, until it gets to the last step in the chain, as Factor 2 triggers Factor 1. The end result of this chain is that a mesh of **protein** and fibres is formed, trapping blood cells and forming a clot that stops any more blood escaping.

If any of the chemicals in the chain are missing, the whole chain breaks down and the blood cannot clot properly. The most common type of haemophilia is A, where Factor 8 is missing; in type B, Factor 9 is missing. In mild haemophilia the level of Factor 8 is lower than normal; in severe cases, it may be completely absent.

Detecting haemophilia

Severe haemophilia is often detected in young babies because they bruise very easily. As they grow older, they may begin to bleed into their joints. This is very painful and can stop the joints forming properly, resulting in disability. Milder forms of haemophilia may not be diagnosed until the child is older, when bleeding from a minor cut continues for longer than is normal.

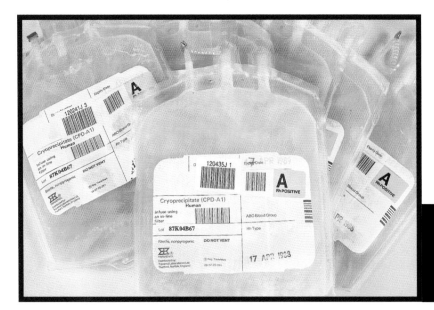

Blood tests will determine the amount of Factor 8 in the blood, and give an indication of the severity of the disease.

These blood products are rich in the blood clotting Factor 8, used to help control haemophilia.

Treatment

Until recent years, there was no treatment for haemophilia and it could be a very disabling disease. Now, Factor 8 can be extracted from blood and injected into patients to prevent uncontrolled bleeding. During the 1980s, many haemophiliacs became infected with AIDS from donated blood containing the HIV virus. Strict controls are now in place to prevent this happening again. Blood is screened very carefully to make sure that it does not contain any infectious agents and, as an extra precaution, all stocks of Factor 8 are specially treated to kill any HIV virus that may be present. Additionally, scientists have now found ways of producing Factor 8 in the laboratory. This does not use blood from donors, and therefore carries no risk of infection.

Inheriting haemophilia

Haemophilia is an inherited disease. This means that it is passed from one generation to the next. Looking at patterns in family trees over many generations has helped scientists to understand how haemophilia is inherited. It is very rare for a woman to be a haemophiliac, but she can be a 'carrier', which means that her sons can be haemophiliacs.

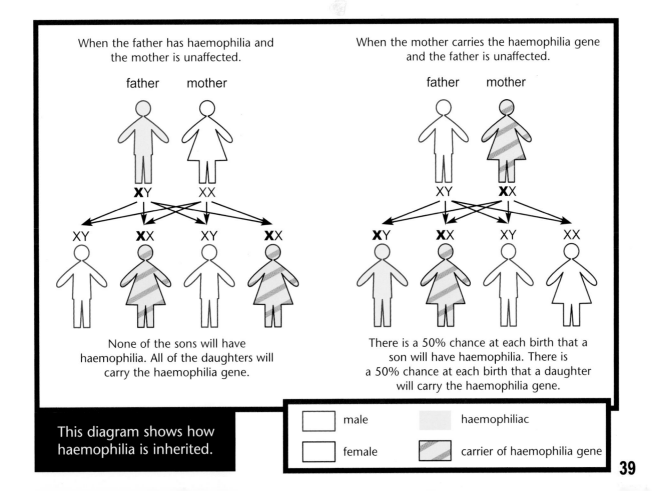

When the father has haemophilia and the mother is unaffected.

When the mother carries the haemophilia gene and the father is unaffected.

father   mother

father   mother

XY   XX

XY   **X**X

XY   **X**X   XY   **X**X

XY   **X**X   XY   XX

None of the sons will have haemophilia. All of the daughters will carry the haemophilia gene.

There is a 50% chance at each birth that a son will have haemophilia. There is a 50% chance at each birth that a daughter will carry the haemophilia gene.

□ male   ▨ haemophiliac

□ female   ▨ carrier of haemophilia gene

This diagram shows how haemophilia is inherited.

BLOOD DISORDERS

Blood plays an important part in maintaining the functioning of every organ and tissue in the body. Any disorder of the blood itself can therefore affect the rest of the body. There are a variety of different things that can affect the blood.

Anaemia

Anaemia means that a person's blood cannot carry as much oxygen as it should. It makes a patient feel tired and lifeless, and their skin often looks pale. There are several possible causes of anaemia:

- heavy loss of blood, from injury or internal bleeding
- lack of iron, because the diet does not contain enough iron or because the body does not absorb it properly. Good sources of iron include meat (especially liver), eggs, shellfish, some vegetables, beans, nuts and fruits.
- failure of **bone marrow** to function properly, usually due to poison or radiation
- bursting of red blood cells e.g. by **malarial parasite**
- immature red blood cells due to lack of **vitamin** B12. Good sources of vitamin B12 include meat, milk, cheese and eggs.

The most common cause of anaemia is lack of iron and this is usually treated by iron tablets or iron injections. Because some of the major sources of iron are meats, vegetarians and vegans have to be particularly careful to ensure that their diet includes enough iron.

Leukaemia

Leukaemia is a cancer of the blood. The two main forms of leukaemia are:

- myeloid leukaemia – starts in the bone marrow
- lymphocytic (or lymphoblastic) leukaemia – starts in the **lymphatic system**.

Either type may be acute (developing very rapidly) or chronic (developing more slowly, and less serious). In acute leukaemia, two things happen:

- white blood cells do not mature properly so they cannot fight infections
- too many white blood cells are produced so that they clog up the bone marrow, stopping it working properly; they spill into the blood, liver and **spleen** where they cause even more problems.

Patients suffering from leukaemia are often anaemic because their bone marrow is unable to make enough red blood cells. They are susceptible to infections as their white blood cells cannot work properly, and they often bleed and bruise easily because they do not have enough **platelets** to clot the blood.

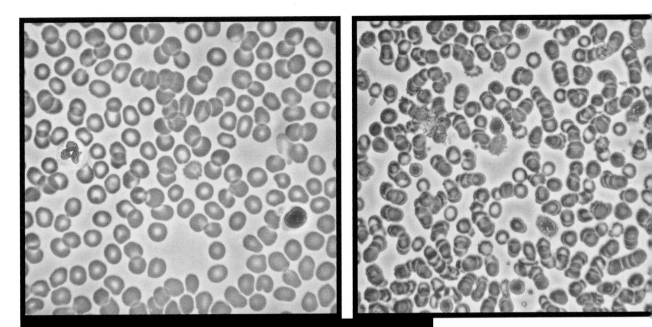

The photograph on the left shows a sample of normal blood. The photograph on the right shows a sample from someone with leukaemia; there are many more white blood cells (shown in blue).

Leukaemia is usually treated by chemotherapy – drugs to kill the white blood cells. The bone marrow can then grow again, and operate properly to produce normal white blood cells. **Radiotherapy** can also be used to stop production of white blood cells.

Bone marrow transplants are sometimes used as well, if a suitable donor is available. A brother or sister is the best donor, as their cells are likely to be most closely matched to the patient's. This minimizes the risk of rejection of the transplant, and the risk of the transplanted cells attacking the patient's body.

Bone marrow transplant

The patient's bone marrow is first treated with drugs and radiation. Bone marrow is sucked out of the donor's pelvic bones, and then filtered to remove unwanted cells before being injected into the patient's bloodstream. The transplanted cells find their way into the patient's bone marrow, where they take over the function of producing healthy blood cells.

There is not always a suitable donor within the family, so searches have to be made countrywide and sometimes worldwide. Registers of people willing to donate are kept, with details of their tissue types, so that when a donor is needed they can be contacted quickly.

SICKLE CELL ANAEMIA

Sickle cell anaemia is an inherited disease that affects red blood cells, causing difficulties with transport of oxygen around the body. It is more common among some population groups than others, and can be diagnosed by a simple blood test.

Sickle cell anaemia affects the red blood cells. The **haemoglobin molecules** become long and stiff, bending the red blood cells into a sickle shape. These sickled cells do not carry or release as much oxygen as normal red blood cells do, and they also burst easily. New red blood cells cannot be formed as quickly as the sickled cells burst, and so the person becomes **anaemic**.

Treatment

People with sickle cell anaemia may not know they have the condition until they suffer a 'crisis'. The sickled cells block small blood vessels, preventing normal blood flow and causing pain, especially in the bones and joints. During a crisis, a person will be given plenty of fluids, and oxygen if needed. Transfusions of healthy red blood cells can be given, although the patient will continue to produce their own sickled cells too. A **bone marrow** transplant can be very beneficial, if a suitable donor is available.

Because of the poor oxygen transport, other symptoms of sickle cell anaemia include tiredness, weakness and an increased likelihood of catching coughs, colds and other infections.

Much of the treatment for sickle cell anaemia can be carried out at home. Parents need to help young children, but teenagers can often deal with their medicines and treatment themselves. Medicines need to be pumped into the body regularly. The medicine can be delivered via a

This photomicrograph shows the deformed blood cells of sickle cell anaemia.

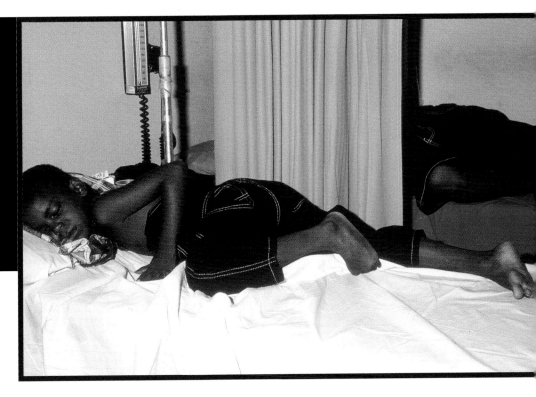

Sickle cell anaemia is most common in areas of the world where malaria is prevalent. This African boy is receiving hospital treatment for the condition.

needle, attached to a small portable pump by a length of flexible tubing, so the patient can move around during the treatment. Some may use the pump overnight, so they receive their medicine while they sleep.

Some patients need **blood transfusions** and this means a trip to hospital. Healthy blood from donors can help to reduce the effects of the sickle cell anaemia. For children and teenagers, this can mean a lot of time off school. To ensure they do not fall behind with their work, facilities are usually available so that they can study and do homework while they are at the hospital.

Sickle cell anaemia and malaria

Sickle cell anaemia is most common among people who live in areas where **malaria** is **prevalent** – particularly people of African and Caribbean descent, but also in those from India, Pakistan, the Middle East and Eastern Mediterranean areas.

Sickle cell trait is not the same as sickle cell anaemia. It rarely causes any health problems and, in countries where malaria is common, it can actually be beneficial – the blood contains high levels of potassium and this kills the **malarial parasites**.

WHAT CAN GO WRONG WITH MY HEART AND BLOOD?

This book has explained the function of the heart and blood, why they are important and how they can be affected by injury and illness. This page summarizes some of the problems that can affect young people. It also gives you information about how each problem is treated.

Many problems can also be avoided by good health behaviour. This is called prevention. Taking regular exercise and getting plenty of rest are important, as is eating a balanced diet. This is important in your teenage years, when your body is still developing. The table shows you some of the ways you can prevent injury and illness.

Remember, if you think something is wrong with your body, you should always talk to a trained medical professional, like a doctor or a school nurse. Regular medical check-ups are an important part of maintaining a healthy body.

Illness or injury	Cause	Symptoms	Prevention	Treatment
Anaemia	Heavy loss of blood, lack of iron and vitamins, red blood cell problem.	Feeling tired and lifeless. Skin usually looks pale.	A diet providing plenty of iron and vitamins, found in meat, cheese, eggs and milk.	Iron intake can be boosted by iron tablets or iron injections. Medical causes such as blood loss need specialist treatment.
High blood pressure	Hardening and thickening of artery walls, reducing their elasticity.	Virtually no symptoms, so it is often undetected until serious, or during an examination for another problem.	Maintain a healthy weight with a balanced diet and regular exercise. Avoid smoking cigarettes.	Weight loss if obese. Increase in exercise. Low fat diet. Stop smoking, and reduce stress. Drug treatment if these measures are not effective.

Illness or injury	Cause	Symptoms	Prevention	Treatment
Raynaud's disease	Constriction of arterioles in fingers and toes, usually in response to cold, restricting blood supply.	Fingers and toes turn white and cold for a few minutes or longer. Intense pain is felt as they warm up and blood rushes back in.	Keep hands and feet well wrapped up in warm gloves and socks to avoid temperature drop. Avoid moving suddenly from very hot to very cold conditions.	No actual cure, but some special gloves and socks are available with in-built warming systems to prevent extreme cooling.
Varicose veins	Stretching and twisting of veins as valves become weak, often caused by smoking or lack of exercise. Jobs which involve standing for long periods can also be a factor.	Dark, knotty threads visible beneath the skin. Swelling, pain and cramps in the lower legs.	Regular exercise. Avoid smoking cigarettes.	Wearing elastic stockings can prevent swelling. More serious cases may need drugs or surgery.
Phlebitis	Injury or infection of a vein leading to inflammation.	Swelling and discomfort. A red streak may appear along the line of the vein.	Follow general guidelines for good health – eat a balanced diet, take regular exercise and avoid smoking.	Rest and elastic stockings to reduce swelling. Painkillers. Antibiotics to clear up infection if present.

Further reading

Horrible Science, Blood, Bones and Body Bits, Nick Arnold, Tony de Saulles (Scholastic Hippo, 1996)
The Human Machine, The Power Pack: All about your heart, lungs and circulation, Sarah Angliss, Graham Rosewarne (Illustrator) (Belitha Press, 1999)
Human Physiology and Health, David Wright (Heinemann Educational, 2000)
Look at Your Body, Blood, Steve Parker (Franklin Watts, 1996)

GLOSSARY

aerobic using oxygen

anaemia condition where the amount of haemoglobin in the blood is reduced

anaerobic not using oxygen

antibiotics drugs used to fight infections. They destroy micro-organisms, such as bacteria or fungi, but are not effective against viruses.

aorta main artery carrying blood away from the heart

arteriole blood vessel formed by the branching of an artery

artery large blood vessel carrying blood away from the heart

atrium one of the upper chambers of the heart

bacteria type of micro-organism

bacterial infection invasion of body tissue by bacteria, which then reproduce themselves within the tissue

blood clot clump of blood cells and other debris that may block a blood vessel and prevent blood circulating freely

blood transfusion transfer of blood from one person to another

bone marrow soft tissue at the centre of some bones, where blood cells may be produced and fat may be stored

capillary very fine blood vessel

carbohydrate nutrient that is broken down to release energy

cardiac to do with the heart

cholesterol fatty substance

chromosome part of the genetic material found in every cell in the body

circulation movement of blood around the body

collagen protein that makes up many structural parts of the body

defect fault that prevents something working properly

deoxygenated without oxygen

embolism blood clot that blocks an artery

enzyme protein that causes or speeds up chemical reactions

fibrin protein that is involved in the process of blood clotting

genetic passing of characteristics from one generation to the next

grafted attached to

haemoglobin molecule that carries oxygen in the blood

haemophilia hereditary condition in which blood does not clot properly

hereditary can be passed on from one generation to the next

hormones chemicals made in the body. They travel around the body in the blood and affect organs and tissues in a variety of ways.

immune system body's defence mechanisms against infection and disease

local anaesthetic drug given to make a part of the body numb

lymphatic system network of vessels and glands that forms the body's main drainage system and is also involved with immunity

malaria disease caused by infection from a micro-organism transmitted by mosquitos

malarial parasite micro-organism that causes malaria (see above)

membrane thin covering layer of tissue

mineral one of a number of chemicals needed by the body in very small amounts, for example: calcium and iron

molecule one or more atoms joined together. Atoms are the smallest amount of a substance that can be found.

nutrient part of our food that the body can use for energy, growth or repair

oxygenated with oxygen

pericardium membrane around the heart

plasma liquid part of blood

platelets particles involved in blood clotting

prevalent common or widespread

protein complex chemical that is a component of many of the body's structures

pulmonary to do with the lungs

pulse flow of blood through the arteries felt with each heartbeat

radiotherapy treatment with large doses of X-rays or other radiation to kill cells

septum strong wall that separates the two sides of the heart

solute solid that can be dissolved in a liquid

spleen large abdominal organ involved in the formation and destruction of blood cells

stroke blockage of an artery affecting the blood supply to the brain

systemic to do with the whole body

tendency trend or likelihood

valve flap of tissue that prevents backflow of blood

vein large blood vessel carrying blood back to the heart

ventricle one of the lower chambers of the heart

virus very small micro-organism that can cause infection

vitamin one of a number of complicated chemicals needed by the body in very small amounts, for example: vitamin C

INDEX